Just
SMILE
at least you woke today!

Todd Burton, Jr.

Copyright © 2023

Todd Burton, Jr.

All rights reserved.

ISBN:

DEDICATION

This book is dedicated to anyone going through any struggle in life. We live in a world where social media has become our biggest form of media. Which can cause people to be more insecure or not as confident in their everyday life because of the influences of society.

ACKNOWLEDGMENTS

This book would not have been possible without three angels I was fortunate to have in my life. First, I would like to thank my Uncle Andre. Your energy was contagious, and I never seen you in a bad mood. It's like you treated everyday like a celebration. Grandpa Joey, your carefree attitude always made it easy to be in your presence. A big man with an even bigger heart. Being the other only child in our family, I always knew you could understand. The best for last Grandma Louise. No matter your age, your heart was always youthful and full of joy. The only person I knew who fed squirrels every morning. But just like when you see the sun and feel it's going to be a great day, that's how I felt every time she wore her favorite color yellow.

Just SMILE at least you woke up today!

Life is the best ride Disney will never make!

Just SMILE at least you woke up today!

Consistency might bore you, but the results won't.

Just SMILE at least you woke up today!

If you can't grasp the idea of something it was never meant for you to hold.

Just SMILE at least you woke up today!

My glass is always half full.

Just SMILE at least you woke up today!

If you keep time close, you won't have to look for it.

Just SMILE at least you woke up today!

Brutal honesty will always make the record skip, especially if you are used to being lied to.

Just SMILE at least you woke up today!

I don't see obstacles only challenges.

Just SMILE at least you woke up today!

Insults are just words that only hurt if they apply, if they don't then they just sound ignorant.

Just SMILE at least you woke up today!

In life you can't please everyone. But you better make your child happy, they actually matter.

Just SMILE at least you woke up today!

If you started at the finish line, don't rerun the race. Just register for a new one.

Just SMILE at least you woke up today!

If you do something dumb and I apologize for it, it has nothing to do with you, I should have known better.

Just SMILE at least you woke up today!

Don't just show the end result, show them the grind it took to get there.

Just SMILE at least you woke up today!

If it offends you then it applies, but if it doesn't apply continue to pay it no mind.

Just SMILE at least you woke up today!

People will get annoyed by how good your energy is, keep being annoying.

Just SMILE at least you woke up today!

Most opinions are nothing but hate and halitosis.

Just SMILE at least you woke up today!

Don't ever suppress your ego to make insecure people feel comfortable. Because those same people will start to look at you, like you're one of them. Don't insult yourself.

Just SMILE at least you woke up today!

I trust people as far as I can throw them, but I never been a wrestler.

Just SMILE at least you woke up today!

I have never been easter egg hunting so why would I put all my eggs in one basket.

Just SMILE at least you woke up today!

Don't burn bridges, just take an alternate route.

Just SMILE at least you woke up today!

Your inner peace will bother people, like it's a crime to be chill. Weirdo's!

People will copy others because what they are doing is easy to comprehend. If they don't copy, don't worry. They most likely don't have the mental capability to grasp the concept or it's just too intelligible for them.

Just SMILE at least you woke up today!

Be a flower that gets picked for the bouquet not the one left in the garden.

Just SMILE at least you woke up today!

Positive vibes help the soul glow.

Just SMILE at least you woke up today!

The higher you climb; the altitude makes it tougher to breathe. That's why success and mountain climbing isn't for everyone.

Just SMILE at least you woke up today!

When you are born to lead, you don't care to follow.

Just SMILE at least you woke up today!

It's truly hard to believe, it's easier to act like you do.

Just SMILE at least you woke up today!

There's a huge difference in thinking you know and actually knowing.

Just SMILE at least you woke up today!

I'm trying to set the bar; they rather play limbo.

Just SMILE at least you woke up today!

If you ever lose a friend for asking an honest question, they were never your friend to begin with.

Just SMILE at least you woke up today!

No one can sell you anything unless
you buy it, dreams included.

Just SMILE at least you woke up today!

The loser worries about the winner, while the winner only worries about winning.

Just SMILE at least you woke up today!

Some choose quantity over quality. I rather have a quantity of quality.

Just SMILE at least you woke up today!

Why bother to ride waves when you can be the ocean.

Just SMILE at least you woke up today!

People are like flowers. Too much sun can damage their growth and too much water can drown them. They need time to breathe, and people need space.

Just SMILE at least you woke up today!

There are many things that take maximum effort to accomplish, minding your business is not one of them.

Words are like clothes. If you don't know how to put them together, then you aren't saying shit and you don't have any drip.

Just SMILE at least you woke up today!

Some people hear and react, while others listen and respond.

Just SMILE at least you woke up today!

I'm living, always better than dying!

ABOUT THE AUTHOR

Todd Burton, Jr. is an American author from Lynn, Massachusetts. A graduate from Endicott College, some might call him a renaissance man. Being a father, an athlete, educator, coach, and co-host of a local podcast allows him to be a positive role model and influence in his community. He created this book to help motivate and inspire people who aren't as fortunate to have positive influences in their lives.

Made in the USA
Middletown, DE
18 February 2025